DODD, MEAD WONDERS BOOKS include WONDERS OF:

ALLIGATORS AND CROCODILES.
   Blassingame
ANIMAL NURSERIES. Berrill
BARNACLES. Ross and Emerson
BAT WORLD. Lavine
BEYOND THE SOLAR SYSTEM.
   Feravolo
BISON WORLD. Lavine and Scuro
CACTUS WORLD. Lavine
CAMELS. Lavine
CARIBOU. Rearden
CORALS AND CORAL REEFS.
   Jacobson and Franz
CROWS. Blassingame
DINOSAUR WORLD. Matthews
DONKEYS. Lavine and Scuro
EAGLE WORLD. Lavine
FLY WORLD. Lavine
FROGS AND TOADS. Blassingame
GEESE AND SWANS. Fegely
GEMS. Pearl
GRAVITY. Feravolo
HAWK WORLD. Lavine
HERBS. Lavine
HUMMINGBIRDS. Simon
JELLYFISH. Jacobson and Franz
KELP FOREST. Brown
LLAMAS. Perry
LIONS. Schaller
MARSUPIALS. Lavine
MEASUREMENT. Lieberg

MONKEY WORLD. Berrill
MOSQUITO WORLD. Ault
OWL WORLD. Lavine
PELICAN WORLD. Cook and Schreiber
PRAIRIE DOGS. Chace
PRONGHORN. Chace
RACCOONS. Blassingame
ROCKS AND MINERALS. Pearl
SEA GULLS. Schreiber
SEA HORSES. Brown
SEALS AND SEA LIONS. Brown
SPIDER WORLD. Lavine
SPONGES. Jacobson and Pang
STARFISH. Jacobson and Emerson
STORKS. Kahl
TERNS. Schreiber
TERRARIUMS. Lavine
TREE WORLD. Cosgrove
TURTLE WORLD. Blassingame
WILD DUCKS. Fegely
WOODS AND DESERT AT NIGHT.
   Berrill
WORLD OF THE ALBATROSS. Fisher
WORLD OF BEARS. Bailey
WORLD OF HORSES. Lavine and
   Casey
WORLD OF SHELLS. Jacobson and
   Emerson
WORLD OF WOLVES. Berrill
YOUR SENSES. Cosgrove

WONDERS OF
CAMELS

SIGMUND A. LAVINE
Illustrated with photographs and old prints

DODD, MEAD & COMPANY, NEW YORK

For Irma—
whose hospitality could transform a
caravansary into an elegant hotel

PICTURE CREDITS

Illustrations courtesy of: American Museum of Natural History, 6, 34, 42, 51, 57, 59; American Spice Trade Association, 21; *Ancient Peoples*, William C. Morey, American Book Company, 32, 64, 65, 66, 67, 68; Australian Information Service, 41, 58, 60–61 *bottom*, 75, 76; British Airways, 9, 15 *right*, 23, 39, 43, 62; British Museum, 12, 17 *right*, 55, 56; Harper's Weekly, 72; Imperial War Museum, London, 70; Israel Bureau of Tourism, 13, 45, 53; Ted Lewin, 2, 38, 73; Library of Congress, 71; Metropolitan Museum of Art, 16; Metropolitan Museum of Art, Francis M. Weld Fund, 1950, 10; Pakistan International Airlines, 35, 49.

1   2   3   4   5   6   7   8   9   10

Library of Congress Cataloging in Publication Data

Lavine, Sigmund A
   Wonders of camels.

   Includes index.
   SUMMARY: Discusses the physical characteristics, evolution, species, and lore of camels, and their relationship to man.
   1.   Camels—Juvenile literature.   [1.   Camels]
I.   Title.
QL737.U54L37   599′.736   78–22436
ISBN 0–396–07670–X

CONTENTS

1
CAMEL LORE

". . . there are countless stories spread."—Towne

Man and camel have been associated for at least four thousand years. Over the centuries they have trudged side by side across burning seas of sand carrying the treasures of the East to western markets. Their unmarked routes stretched from oasis to oasis where water could be found and stands of wind-bent palms provided some relief from the intense heat of the cruel sun. Camels and their masters have also endured sub-zero weather and other hardships for hundreds of years while clambering over rock-strewn mountain passes in central Asia. But camels have not served only as plodding beasts of burden or ungainly mounts. Nomadic tribesmen riding camels bred for speed and stamina have long raided passing caravans and plundered settlements set on the edge of deserts. Camels also have played an important part in modern warfare just as they bore spear- and sword-wielding warriors to victory on many a battlefield in ancient times.

Bactrian camel photographed on a Museum of Natural History Expedition

Old print of a Muslim praying in the desert. Note the camel saddle and bridle.

Despite their ancient alliance, the camel and its masters have not had a close relationship over the centuries. To be sure, individuals have praised the speed and stamina of their animals, but the majority of camel drivers have considered their charges stupid, untrustworthy, and malicious. The camel's evil reputation has branded it as an obnoxious beast in fable, proverb, and superstition. Yet it is often honored in tradition and legend.

When mounted or saddled, camels not only express their displeasure by grunting and groaning but also make horrible faces. These grimaces have annoyed man ever since the camel was first tamed. Devout Muslims maintain that camels have good reason to look at their masters with disdain. According to Islamic lore, the prophet Mohammed confided the Secret of Secrets—the hundredth name of Allah—to the faithful camel that carried him safely into exile when his life was endangered. From that time to this, so the story goes, the Secret of Secrets has been handed down from one camel to another. When a camel looks at a human who lacks its knowledge, the animal feels superior and its face twists into a supercilious sneer.

When praying, Moslems recite the ninety-nine names of Allah. During their prayers they use strings of beads fashioned from camel bones. There are one hundred beads—a terminal bead called Imam (leader) and ninety-nine others—each representing one of Allah's names.

Despite the honored role the camel plays in the history and practice of Islamism, camel owners throughout the Middle East (where many Muslims live) link the camel with evil. At the same time it is widely held that camels are preyed upon by various demoniacal creatures. *Abl at-atrab*, the supernatural beings who live just below the surface of the Sahara Desert, do the most harm to camels. Disguised as whirling pillars of sand, these fiends cause the animals to trip and break a leg. To thwart the unearthly imps that plague their beasts, camel drivers fasten amulets made of blue cloth or blue beads to a camel's saddle, neck, or tail.

Note the decorations on these modern-day camels, their saddles and neck reins.

This leaf from a sixteenth-century Persian manuscript depicts a camel carrying the coffin of Fatima, daughter of Mohammed, founder of Islamism. In colors, tempera and gold on paper.

In Arabia, the superstitious claim that practitioners of black magic often assume camel form. But in Morocco camel bones are hung on houses to protect the inhabitants from the evil eye. Some Moroccans hold that Aucha Kandid, a wicked water witch who lures men by appearing as a beautiful maid, has the feet of a camel.

From North Africa to Armenia, tribal taletellers recount how camels were created from devils or from the eyes of jinn, the malicious nature demons of Arabic tradition that supposedly have miraculous power. Bedouins consider a camel the most valuable of sacrifices. So did the ancient Iranians and the Arabs of the Holy Land. The latter sacrificed camels to mark the death of important people. Camels were also presented to religious shrines by individuals who wished to express gratitude for restored health or successful business ventures. Such camels were held sacred by tribesmen living in the Horn of Africa. But no camel was considered holy by the Jews or by the Copts (members of the early Christian Church in Egypt). Both the Jews and the Copts labeled the camel an unclean beast.

On the other hand, the camel was held in high esteem by the Persian followers of Zoroaster, founder of Zoroastrianism—a religion that maintains that the forces of good and evil wage continuous warfare. There were two reasons why Zoroaster's disciples respected the camel. Not only is Zoroaster's name compounded from the ancient Persian word for camel but also Ahura Madza (the spirit of wisdom living in eternal light) gave Zoroaster a camel.

Because the Persians came in contact with Arabic folklore after they were converted to Islamism their attitude toward the camel changed. For example, they accepted the belief that one should never pray where camels rest because such places are the haunts of devils. The Persians also developed their own camel superstitions, as well as borrowing those of others. Thus every camel driver in the country knew of the monstrous ghoul with a weird voice that lurked in lonely areas in the guise of a camel and ate lost travelers.

Traditionally the three kings, Caspar, Melchior, and Balthazar, rode camels as they followed the star to Bethlehem. 'Tis claimed the Magi were grateful to the mounts that carried both themselves and their gifts to the infant Jesus. Therefore, Spanish youngsters who receive their Christmas presents from the three kings on January 6, the Day of Kings (*Dia de Reyes*), are not surprised to find wisps of grass as well as playthings in the shoes they left outside the doors of their houses the previous night. The children know that the grass is for the Wise Men's camels.

No medieval artist made more spirited drawings of animals than Vittore Pisano, commonly called Pisanello. This detailed sketch of a camel illustrates Pisanello's outstanding skill as a draughtsman.

Actually, compared to the ox and the donkey, the camel has little association with Christianity. However, a medieval bestiary credits Adam with naming the camel in the Garden of Eden. The unknown monk who wrote the bestiary claims that Adam chose "camel" because the animal kneels down when being loaded. Adam—so the monk states—derived camel from *cam*, the Greek word for low. In case some readers found fault with this explanation, the good monk also noted that Adam, observing the creature's hump, concocted camel from the Greek *camur* (curved). But the author of the bestiary does not tell his readers how Adam learned Greek!

Lexicographers—compilers of dictionaries—have traced the origin of the word camel to the Semitic *gamel* or *hamel* (carrying a burden). In those Arabic-speaking lands where camels

12

are common, youngsters may be called *jamal* (camel) rather than by their own names. This is done to confuse the evil spirits who know the names of those they wish to harm. Desert nomads who greatly prize racing camels employ the word camel as a term of endearment when addressing their loved ones. But Germans are not paying a compliment when they call an individual *kamel*. It means he is ungainly, clumsy, and stupid. In circus slang, a camel punk is a boy hired to water animals in the show's menagerie.

Camels have been exhibited in zoos for hundreds of years. Centuries before camels were used as beasts of burden in Egypt they were displayed in temple menageries throughout that country. Both giant and parti-colored camels were included in the animal collection of Haroun al Roschid, who plays an important part in the legendary *Arabian Nights*. Teams of camels were among the war trophies Alexander the Great displayed to the Greek people. Roman generals sent hundreds of camels to Rome

Above Jerusalem, a camel races along the summit of the Mount of Olives. Note saddle and bridle; camel is guided by a long stick.

where they were used in the gladiatorial games or exhibited as curiosities. Besides being shown in Rome, camels were shipped to the outposts of the Roman Empire. Camel bones dating back to the first century B.C. have been unearthed in the ruins of the Roman theater at Vindonisse in Switzerland.

Charlemagne—who established three zoos in the eighth century—kept camels, as did the thirteenth-century Holy Roman Emperor Frederick III. An outstanding naturalist, Frederick was accompanied by elephants, lions, monkeys, and both one- and two-humped camels during his extensive journeys.

In 1622, Ferdinand II of the Medici family imported several one-humped camels and turned them loose to graze on the plains near Pisa, Italy. The herd prospered and approximately two hundred camels roamed the countryside around Pisa until the outbreak of World War II, when they were shot and eaten by German occupation troops.

No one knows whether or not the Germans drank large quantities of wine while feasting on the descendants of Ferdinand's camels. If they did, there was no reason for a single soldier to become intoxicated—folklore holds that one can consume large amounts of wine with no ill effects providing a small amount of camel saliva is mixed with it.

Curing drunkenness is but one of the many attributes ancient lore assigns to the camel. In earlier times, Turkish doctors compounded camel bones into many of their prescriptions. For centuries, camel-owning peoples have rubbed the throats and chests of children suffering from whooping cough with camel grease. (A child's *whoop* supposedly sounds like the grunt of a camel). However, certain tribes do not consider camel grease an infallible remedy for whooping cough. They insist the only cure is to hang a camel's windpipe on the neck of the sufferer. They recommend the same remedy for a case of hiccups.

This old print of the "Land of Egypt" was made years before the strikingly similar photograph.

The Egyptians believed that a piece of cloth rubbed against their ruler's camel and worn as an amulet would keep one healthy. Yet, oddly enough, the Egyptians thought that camels were accident prone. In fact, they were convinced that if one did not say "God preserve us" on meeting a camel, the animal would eventually fall and break a leg.

When plague devastated the countryside in ancient Arabia, a camel was led through every street of a town in hopes that the pestilence would be transferred to the animal. The camel was then strangled in a sacred place—and the town was supposedly rid of the plague.

Throughout North Africa, camel's teeth were widely used in primitive medical preparations. Camel owners not only thought

15

that many sicknesses could be cured if one ground up a camel's molar, burnt it, and inhaled the smoke but also were convinced that this procedure provided protection from the evil eye. Even today, certain North Africans hang a camel's tooth from their necks to ward off disease and also to repel sorcerers. Even those individuals who are healthy and have no fear of black magic often make use of a ground-up camel's tooth. Placed in the food of a youth or maid, it assures love.

Male camels have no love for one another and will fight at the slightest provocation. Their pugnaciousness was formerly taken advantage of in Turkey where camel wrestling was a popular sport. The animals were trained to cross necks and attempt to force their opponents to the ground.

LEFT: *Made in India during the eigthteenth century, this solid gold camel supports a miniature saddle painted on ivory.* CENTER: *Crafted in Persia approximately three thousand years ago, this two-humped bronze camel is partly hollow.* RIGHT: *Some seventeen hundred years ago, a Syrian silversmith created this representation of a camel. It is unusual because it carries two riders.*

16

Assyrian "Black Obelisk of Shalmaneser II" and photo of detail from same. Camels are identified in the inscription (in cuneiform) as "Camels whose backs are doubled."

Fighting camels are a popular motif in Muslim art. But long before Mohammed described Al Jassasa, the colossal beast with camel's feet that will mark the faces of the faithful with Moses' rod on Judgment Day, artists were depicting camels. Their work ranges from crude representations of camels etched on stones by primitive man to exquisite jeweled figurines fashioned by master craftsmen.

There is as wide a variation in the materials used by artists to create camels as there is in the quality of their work. Camels have been fashioned from bronze, clay, copper, gold, porcelain, silver, stone, and wood. Delineations of the camel range in size from carved precious stones to massive bas-reliefs designed for city walls. During the Ming Dynasty (A.D. 1368–1666) when the emperors of China encouraged the development of the arts, the royal tombs outside the city of Peking were decorated with huge kneeling camels. While these animals are majestic, no sculptured camels are more lifelike than those chiseled by Assyrian artisans during the reign of Assurbanipal (669–633 B.C.)

17

Much early pottery is decorated with crudely executed camels. Excellent likenesses of camels appear on coins struck by cities along ancient caravan routes. Spirited camels also march across the colorful textiles woven by the Copts and on antique Persian porcelain bowls.

Shortly after A.D. 1400, an unknown miniature painter living in Vienna compiled a pattern book for artists. One of the drawings in this volume is of a camel's head. While the drawing is lifelike, it cannot compare to Rembrandt's sketch of a resting camel.

During the Middle Ages when religious themes dominated art, most masters of the brush painted camels. Typical of these paintings is "Journey of the Magi," created by Gozzoli in the fifteenth century. The camels in this canvas are drawn extremely well. Gozzoli, an accomplished artist, drew them from life. His models were the camels in the Medici family's private menagerie at Florence.

Camels carry a heavy load in literature. Some of the "facts" early naturalists set down about camels make as colorful reading as the Asiatic fables in which the camel is outwitted by Jackal or Monkey. For example, the famous Greek philosopher Aristotle claimed that the camel "likes turbid and thick water, and will never drink from a stream until he has tramped it into a turbid condition." This belief lasted until relatively modern times, one authority maintaining that camels "have their best delight in drinking when as by foote they trouble the water." There is a slight connection between this conviction and the Arab tradition that a camel haunts a spring in Ramallah near the city of Jerusalem. The credulous claim that if the water in the spring is low, the camel is drinking; if the water is muddy, they say the camel is wallowing; and if the spring makes a murmuring noise, the camel is thought to be moaning.

The Nile—low water and high. The belief that camels liked to drink

muddy water persisted for years. It was also a common misconception that the reason camels could travel long distances through desert lands was because they stored water in their humps.

Camels are leading characters in the long epics recited by the Baluchi tribesmen of India. These tales detail the bloody battles fought for the hand of Helen, a beautiful maiden who owned vast herds of camels. Indian literature also contains stories relating the misadventures of attractive princesses who were transformed into ugly camels by wicked wizards. Still other stories describe the deeds of mythical heroes who fly through the sky at tremendous speeds on the backs of winged camels. Hindu tales tell of men turned into camels and doomed to remain in that form unless shot by a certain king.

Literature is crammed with accounts of supernatural camels. According to the Kirghiz who live on the steppes of central Asia, a herd of snow-white camels grazes on the summit of Mustagh Ata, the tallest peak in the Pamir Range.

Legendary camels play an important role in Arabic literature. Traditionally, these animals live in the mysterious land of Wabar which lies somewhere in southern Arabia. If ancient tales are true, the camels of the Wabar are extremely dangerous. This is because they mate with camels belonging to jinn.

Early Arabic poets viewed the camel with mixed emotions. Some compared its speed to the wind sweeping across the desert. Others were not so complimentary. They stressed the ugliness, stubbornness, and meanness of the camel and told of its supposed association with evil.

The first English-speaking poet to mention the camel was probably the unknown author of *Cursor Mundi*—a long religious epic relating the history of the world as recorded in the Old and New Testaments. Written in A.D. 1300, in the northern English dialect of the period, *Cursor Mundi* describes individuals who own camels and those who "no haveth camayle." A few years later, Chaucer (ca. 1343–1400), one of the most important poets of all time, wrote of the "camaille."

Shakespeare and other famous authors make frequent men-

It is impossible to tell whether the camels in this early engraving have one or two humps. However, the chances are excellent that the camels in the caravan shown climbing the mountains in the upper left-hand corner are Bactrians.

tions of the camel. However, modern poets have found little inspiration in the beast. Usually, they ridicule it in a good-natured manner.

With the exception of certain stories in Aesop's *Fables* and a few other tales, both oral and written literature stress the camel's nasty disposition. Thus an Egyptian folktale relates how a camel and a donkey ran away and hid from their master. Although the camel warned his companion to keep quiet, the donkey brayed and they were discovered. While being returned to the stable, the donkey, always lazy, pretended to hurt its leg. Seeing the

21

donkey limp, its owner loaded him onto the camel's back. Eventually, the party passed a ledge and the camel rubbed against the rocks, throwing the donkey to the ground. As the donkey rolled down the hillside the camel bellowed, "Why didn't you keep your mouth shut?"

A favorite story of the Berbers of North Africa deals with a grocer and a potter who hired a camel to carry their wares to market. The grocer packed vegetables in a basket hung on one side of the camel while the potter placed pots in a basket on the other side. On the way to the market the camel kept turning its head in order to eat the vegetables. The potter thought this was very funny but he stopped laughing when the camel stopped at a water hole and knelt to rest. As it did, it leaned on the basket containing the pots and broke them.

This tale is the origin of the Berber idiom "Let's see on what side the camel sits"—an expression used to convince a person not to make a hasty decision. In all probability, the story itself relates to the well-known proverb, "He who laughs last, laughs best."

One of the most famous literary references to the camel is found in the New Testament—"It is easier for a camel to go through the eye of a needle, than for a rich man to enter into the kingdom of God." This is a paraphrase of a proverb common in various forms wherever camels serve man. Meanwhile the Koran—the Muslim scripture—warns that the wicked will not reach Paradise "until a camel passes through the eye of a needle."

This admonition and the proverbs on which it is based may have been inspired by the extremely large needle threaded with rope used to sew camel saddlebags. However, some authorities believe that the idea of a camel passing through a needle stems from the narrow gate camels had to use to enter the city of Jerusalem.

The origin of another Biblical proverb is much easier to trace.

Camel with baskets is led through an Egyptian village.

"To strain at a gnat and swallow a camel" is derived from the custom of straining wine before drinking it, to avoid accidentally swallowing an insect. But the proverb has nothing to do with either insects or wine. It is used to reprimand those who make a difficulty of accepting an idea.

English-speaking peoples say "Give him an inch and he'll take a yard." This is the equivalent of the Arabic "If the camel gets his nose in the tent his body will soon follow." Another proverb has an identical meaning in Arabic, English, Greek, Latin, and Turkish—"The camel desired horns and lost its ears." This seemingly absurd proverb—which probably stems from the belief that camels have poor hearing and the fact that they have relatively shorter ears than most large animals—is based on an ancient tale. In it, the camel asked God for horns. Not only did God deny this request but also He trimmed the camel's ears as a punishment for its presumption. The moral of this proverb is that by seeking too much, one may lose the little he has.

According to the Turks, "Making a fool understand is like making a camel leap a ditch." But no Turkish proverb is as meaningful as "Death is a black camel which kneels at everyone's gate." Here death is represented as a camel that is sure

24

to stop sooner or later before every man's door to receive and bear his body away for burial.

Actually, it would take dozens of books the size of this one merely to list all the proverbs that mention the camel. Indeed, there seems to be no limit to the proverbs derived from the camel's age, color, hump, huge mouth, large eyes, short tail, slit nose, mighty strength, jealousy, stupidity, and nasty disposition. While the Persian "The camel is at your gate" is considered a polite way to tell an individual he is wrong, most camel proverbs are employed for ridicule. For example, in India, those who sing off key are described as "Nightingales like the camel."

Early Arabic astronomers spotted four stars that formed a diamond on the edge of the Milky Way. They named the diamond—which we call the Dolphin—Al-Ka'ud (The Riding Camel). Meanwhile, in the Orient, caravans were using the Pleiades—a cluster of stars in the constellation Taurus—as a "compass" during their journeys. Traditionally, the leader of a caravan could locate the Pleiades with little trouble. Oriental

Oriental folklore holds that when camels kneel to rest, their heads are turned toward the group of stars called the Pleiades.

A caravan overtaken by a sandstorm in the desert

folklore not only maintains that camels can see the Pleiades long before man but also it holds that when camels kneel to rest, their heads are always turned toward this group of stars.

Besides being associated with astronomy, camels are prominent in weather lore. When camels become restless and sniff the air while crossing a desert in Persia, their owners believe a sandstorm is coming. Syrians hold that if one dreams of clouds bigger than a camel, it will not rain. However, throughout central Asia an ancient tale states that storms are caused by three men who ride a camel across the sky. One man beats a drum causing it to thunder, the second waves a scarf which creates lightning, while the third pulls on the reins causing water (saliva) to run from the camel's mouth.

2
MEET THE CAMELS

"Nature has fram'd strange fellows in her time."—Shakespeare

How many humps does a camel have?

Be careful—there is no correct answer to this seemingly simple question. Some camels have two humps while others have but one. Moreover, certain members of the Camelidae family (the alpacas, guanacos, llamas, and vicuñas of South America) lack humps.

Zoologists—students of animal life—have named the single-humped camel *Camelus dromedarius*. Because this animal was probably first domesticated in ancient Arabia, it is commonly called the Arabian camel. It is also known as the dromedary. However, it is incorrect to call all Arabian camels dromedaries. Technically, a dromedary is a special breed of one-humped camel trained to run at top speed while carrying a rider.

The double-humped camel's scientific name is *Camelus bactrianus*, because it may have been domesticated first in Bactria (the classical name of a valley in northern Afghanistan). Popularly called the Bactrian camels, they are more ponderous though not as tall as their single-humped kin. Over the centuries two-humped camels have developed physical characteristics that enable them to work long hours in extremely cold temperatures. Similarly, the Arabian camels have become ideally adapted to life in the desert. The modifications that enable both one- and two-humped camels to thrive in their respective environments are described in Chapter 3.

Until comparatively recent times the majority of zoologists were convinced that Arabian and Bactrian camels were two distinct species. One reason for this belief was the unquestioned assumption that Arabian and Bactrian camels did not interbreed. However, modern investigation has revealed that camel breeders in the Middle East and Asia have mated one-humped and two-humped camels for centuries. It has also been learned that the offspring of such matings are highly prized because they are heavier and more vigorous than either parent.

Today, most authorities consider Arabian and Bactrian camels geographic races of a single species. This is not only because the two interbreed but also because, with the exception of the Bactrian's slightly shorter leg bones, their skeletons are so similar that experts examining fossilized camel bones from areas where both races once lived are unable to tell whether the bones are those of a one- or two-humped camel.

Because of the dissimilarity in the appearance of Arabian and Bactrian camels, early scientists could justify classifying them as two distinct species. But the difference in humps is more apparent than real. Anatomists have discovered that the Arabian camel has an imperfectly developed anterior hump.

CAMEL CAVALCADE

The earliest known ancestor of the modern camel is *Protylopus*, a harelike creature that lived in the subtropical forests

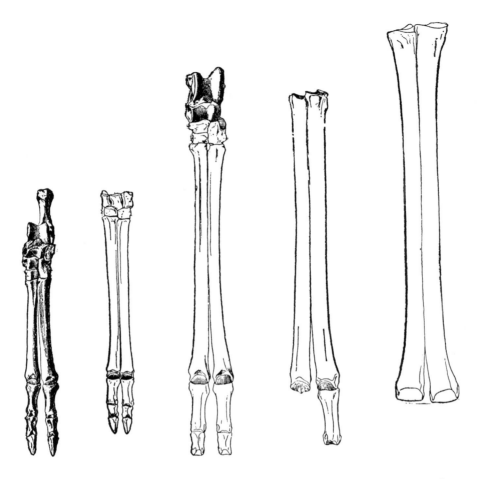

Bones of fossil camels. The one on left is from Protylopus, *on the right,*
Procamelus.

covering North America some forty million years ago. As the
ages passed, *Protylopus'* descendants became larger and their
legs lengthened, enabling them to run rapidly. Some of these
new species resembled sheep or hornless deer. Others were
giraffe-like, having exceptionally long necks and legs. The head
of aptly named *Alticamelus* (high camel) was at least ten feet
above the ground!

Skull of an extinct primitive camel

Paleozoologists—experts in the identification of animal fossils —maintain that the animal we call the camel first appeared about four million years ago in North America. Seeking food, *Camelus* wandered as far north as present-day Alaska and, in time, migrated westward over the land bridge that connected the Old and New World before the Bering Strait was formed.

Meanwhile, large herds of camels continued to graze over the area now known as the Great Plains. Eventually, the immediate ancestors of the alpaca, guanaco, llama, and vicuña trekked southward and finally reached the rugged slopes of the Andes Mountains in South America. Here, their descendants still live. Because these animals closely resemble the humpless camels that lived in Miocene times they can be called "living fossils."

Along with tracing the migrations of the Camelidae, paleo-zoologists have established that camels inhabited North America until comparatively recent times. But, despite their intensive study of hundreds of fossilized camel bones, the experts cannot answer the question, "Why did the humped camels of the New World become extinct?"

TAMING THE ARABIAN CAMEL

Long before camels vanished from their original habitat they had slowly extended their range across the dry belt of the northern hemisphere. Authorities agree that camels reached present-day Romania and the southern part of modern Russia before climatic conditions halted their westward journey. How-

TOP LEFT: *Vicuña.* TOP RIGHT: *Guanaco.* MIDDLE LEFT: *Alpaca.* MIDDLE RIGHT: *Llama.* BOTTOM LEFT: *Arabian camel.* BOTTOM RIGHT: *Bactrian or two-humped camel.*

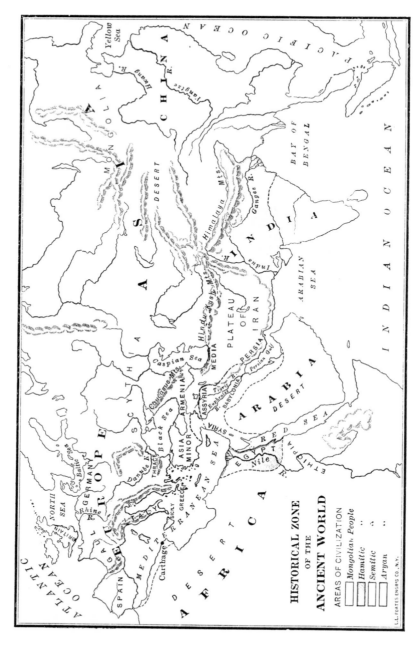

Map of the ancient world

ever, naturalists differ as to when and where the immigrants split into two races: the single-humped and two-humped camels.

While *dromedarius'* origin is obscure, we do know that one-humped camels were not native to the Valley of the Nile. However, they were among the wild animals that inhabited the Arabian peninsula and the lands bordering the Sahara Desert. Proof that good-sized herds of wild camels ranged over these regions less than two thousand years ago is furnished by the writings of Strabo, a Greek geographer who lived in the first century. As in the case of the camel in North America, we can only guess why the herds described by Strabo vanished. It well may be that the animals starved to death. Over the centuries a prolonged drought greatly increased the arid area of the Middle East.

The earliest record of domesticated camels is found in the Bible—the tale of Rebekah watering Abraham's camels. Biblical scholars estimate that this event took place between 1800–1700 B.C. Additional proofs that the Arabian camel has felt the tug of reins for approximately four thousand years is provided by archaeological discoveries that indicate that the Akkadians of northern Babylonia used one-humped camels in warfare as early as 2400 B.C. As a matter of fact, excavations of historical sites throughout the Middle East reveal that several ancient Semitic peoples employed Arabian camels for transport at a very early date.

An Arabian camel decorates a pot fashioned in Egypt about 3500 B.C. Strangely enough, most Egyptians living at the time the camel was painted had never seen a camel. The camel was not common along the Nile until Syrian troops serving the Roman emperor Septimius Severus (A.D. 193–211) patrolled North Africa mounted on camels.

It was not only camel-riding warriors who spread the use of Arabian camels from North Africa to India. Merchants who

A Bactrian camel. Note saddle, stirrup, and peg in nose bridle.

wandered far and wide seeking new markets for the wares their camels carried also paved the way for many peoples to adopt *dromedarius* as a beast of burden.

SADDLING THE BACTRIAN CAMEL

Vast herds of Bactrian camels once grazed widely over central and northwest Asia. However, available evidence only allows us to speculate that the double-humped camel was first

34

brought into the service of man in Bactria. From approximately 1000 B.C. there is a tremendous amount of data confirming that the Bactrian was used in Armenia, Assyria, Persia, and Mesopotamia. Written and pictorial materials show that the residents of these countries employed the two-humped camel not only as a pack and draft animal but also as a mount. Certain authorities also claim the Bactrians were not limited to carrying supplies in time of war but also were ridden by cavalrymen. Incidentally, a group of warriors mounted on camels is called camelry.

Despite the great value of the Bactrian both as a beast of burden and as a mount, the majority of camel-owning peoples discarded the two-humped camel when trade or war brought them into contact with the Arabian camel. This did not happen overnight but, eventually, use of the Bactrian was confined to the colder parts of Asia where the Arabian camel could not survive.

Camel caravan passing through the Khagan Valley near the legendary State of Swat in Pakistan

RIGHT: *Marco Polo.* BELOW: *Old print shows Bactrian mother and baby near a Mongolian hut.*

MONGOLIAN HUT.

Not all Bactrian camels plod across windswept steppes, clamber over snow-covered mountain passes, or live contentedly in zoos. A small herd of Bactrians—the only wild camels in the world—live on the Mongolian side of the Alati Mountains. While it is most likely these animals—mentioned by Marco Polo and early Chinese writers—have interbred with tame camels, they differ greatly from typical Bactrians. Motion pictures taken of the herd show that its members have shorter and lighter coats, are more slender in build, and have smaller humps, ears, and feet than domesticated Bactrians.

3
PHYSICAL CHARACTERISTICS OF THE CAMEL

"But a Camel's all lumpy
And bumpy and humpy . . ."—Carryl

As indicated—with the exception of the slight differences in appearance and special adaptions that enable camels to withstand heat or cold—there is little variation between Arabian and Bactrian camels. Thus, in the pages that follow, unless special attention is directed to a dissimilarity, it should be understood that the physical characteristic being discussed is identical in both one- and two-humped camels.

BODY

The minor distinctions between the skeletons of the two races of camels are of interest only to zoologists. One need not be a scientist to distinguish an Arabian from a Bactrian. Not only

An Arabian camel in a New York zoo in the act of kneeling. This can be disconcerting to new riders.

does the number of humps make identification easy but so does the knowledge that the Arabian camel has thinner legs and a more slender build than the Bactrian camel.

Camels appear to be larger than they actually are due to their thick, woolly fur. The length of a camel's head, neck, and body is approximately ten feet. A full-grown Bactrian stands between six and seven feet at the shoulder; an adult Arabian about six inches shorter. Because Bactrians—which can weigh up to 1400 pounds—have stocky frames, they make excellent pack animals. On the other hand, the lighter bone structure of the Arabian enables it to move much faster than its heavier kin, making it more suitable as a mount.

Both Arabian and Bactrian camels can kneel or rise with a load on their backs. When dropping to the ground, camels bend the front legs, kneel, fold up the hind legs, and fall. To stand, a camel straightens the hind legs and jerks up the front legs. Incidentally, riders dismount just as their mounts fold the hind legs. This can be a most graceful maneuver providing the camel doesn't suddenly decide to stand.

All camels have callosities on the knees, breastbone, and other parts of the body that touch the ground when they kneel. These leather-like patches of skin are not caused by hair being rubbed off but are natural growths that protect the animal from burning itself on hot sand.

The ropelike tufted tails are about eighteen inches long. Normally camels are brown or gray but individuals may range in color from almost white to black. Breeds developed by desert nomads have very light beige or fawn wool coats—the characteristic coloration of animals in arid regions. The coats of Bactrian camels in cold areas are usually deep brown.

An Arabian camel's fur is short and lies close to the body. Bactrians have longer fur—in midwinter it may be ten inches in length—which gives the upper parts of the forelegs a shaggy appearance and hangs like a beard under the animal's neck. In the spring, camels molt. Because the old fur falls out in patches which cling to the body, a shedding camel is best described as "motheaten." But once molting is over a camel looks sleek and streamlined—until its new coat is fully grown.

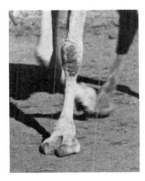

Note the callosity that protects camel from burning sands, also the widespread foot for walking in sand.

LEGS AND FEET

Camels are ungulates—mammals whose toes are enclosed in hoofs. Both races of camels bear their weight equally on the third and fourth (center) toes of each foot. These toes are connected by a thick, elastic cushion-like pad. As a camel moves, the pads spread. As a result, the pads help support Arabian camels in loose sand and serve Bactrian camels as snowshoes. However, neither the widely splayed feet which are set nearly flat on the ground, the padded toes, nor the tough soles are designed for walking through mud. Therefore, loaded camels find it difficult to maintain normal pace when crossing soggy ground.

Over the centuries the feet of camels have been modified. Those employed as pack animals in deserts have soft feet that are often the size of a large plate. While these camels balk at walking on rocky ground, their huge feet enable them to cross over sand without sinking. The feet of camels used to transport goods in rocky areas are smaller and tougher. But irrespective of the size or hardness of their feet, most camels suffer from corns.

The camels in this caravan carry heavy loads across the Sahara.

Despite their mounts' rocking gait, most of these riders seem to be enjoying a trip on "the ship of the desert." However, one young lady appears to be seasick.

Few animals have stronger legs than camels. Extremely powerful muscles in the upper part of the long legs permit camels to pack very heavy loads long distances day after day. A camel can carry a thousand pound load at a speed of approximately three miles an hour. During an eight- to ten-hour working day, a loaded camel travels about twenty-five miles. Racing dromedaries can gallop one hundred miles in a day at an average speed of ten miles an hour.

Camels move both legs on one side of the body forward at the same time. Although this gait is identical with the attractive stride of a pacing horse, camels lack grace because they sway from side to side as they move. Some authorities claim that this rocking motion—which makes inexperienced riders feel seasick—

41

is the source of the camel's nickname "ship of the desert." Other experts do not support this theory. Basing their argument on the Assyrian custom of naming animals according to the place from which they came, these individuals maintain that "ship of the desert" is a mistranslation of the Assyrian "animal brought in a ship from the desert." If this explanation is correct, it confirms the contention of many historians that large numbers of camels were shipped across the Persian Gulf in ancient times.

HUMP

Most animals have an equal layer of fat over the entire body, but camels concentrate their fat in a lump. This lump, composed of pads of fat held together with tough tissue, forms the hump. Arabian camels in good condition have tall stiff humps; those of healthy Bactrian camels are bulbous and squashy. Generally speaking, the hump constitutes approximately one-twentieth of a camel's total weight.

Whenever food is scarce, camels draw on the fat in their humps for energy. Because the humps lack supporting bones, they shrink as the fat is consumed. The hump of a hungry Arabian camel contracts noticeably, while the humps of a starving Bactrian become so flabby that they flop over and hang down the animal's sides. However, if camels that have exhausted

Note flabby humps on some of these Bactrian camels.

Note the eyes, ears, and nose of this Arabian camel.

their stored fat rest for a day or two and are given all the food they can consume, the humps soon regain their normal shape and texture.

EYES, EARS, AND NOSE

Camels have large eyes on the sides of the head. Thick protruding eyebrows act as "sunglasses" while each eye is protected by three eyelids. Long curly eyelashes on the outer two lids shield the eyes from blowing desert sand or the freezing rain of the frigid steppes. Any dust that does get into the eye is wiped off by a thin inner eyelid that "winks" across the eyeball.

The nostrils also have a special adaption to prevent dust, sand, or ice pellets from blowing into them. Special muscles enable camels to close, or partially close, their nostrils at will. Similarly, the small rounded ears, which are set far back on the head, are protected. Because they are covered, both inside and outside, with hair, it is difficult for foreign matter to blow into them. Camels have excellent hearing but many of them are so stubborn and rebellious that they often pretend not to hear commands.

43

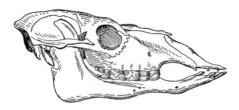

Skull of a camel shows teeth.

Teeth

Camels not only use their strong, sharp teeth to chew food but also employ them as weapons. Because camels can be vicious, their owners may prevent them from biting by placing a muzzle over their large mouths. This is a wise precaution—a camel inflicts a slashing bite that is a far more serious wound than the bite made by the largest dog.

A newborn camel has, along with other teeth, six incisors (cutting teeth) in both the upper and lower jaws. As the baby matures it loses all its upper teeth except the outside incisors. The lost teeth are replaced by a horny structure which works against the spoon-shaped lower incisors when the animal grazes. Because this structure is impervious to thorns, camels can make a banquet of prickly-pear cactus. They also relish alkaline plants other animals find unpalatable. When eating, camels grasp food with the lips, which are modified for pulling leaves and picking twigs. The upper lip is cleft. This cleft not only makes it easier to crop plants but also permits camels to spit with deadly accuracy when annoyed.

However, even the most gentle and best-tempered of camels will never star in a "commercial" for toothpaste. Not only do camels have bad breath but also as they grow older their teeth become stained a deep dirty yellow.

Digestion

Although camels can go without food for considerable periods they have hearty appetites. Specimens kept in zoos and circuses

44

consume eight pounds of grain and hay daily. Working camels rarely enjoy such a rich diet. Most of them are pastured and feed on wild plants.

However, some camel owners do provide their stock with food. These individuals feed their animals dates, grass, oats, and wheat. Perhaps the most unusual "fodder" is fed in the southern part of the Arabian peninsula—dried shark meat and sardines! Actually, a hungry camel will devour anything—"bones, fish, meat, skin, its bridle, and even its owner's tent." In fact, the camel's gluttony is one reason ancient naturalists thought it had five stomachs.

Camels are ruminants—grazing animals that have split hoofs, chew cuds, and have stomachs with several chambers. The camel was the first ruminant to evolve and it differs slightly from other ruminants, which have four compartments in their stomachs. Camels' stomachs have only three compartments.

Most working camels like this one near Jerusalem are pastured and find their own food.

Moreover, camels chew their cuds differently.

Like all ruminants, camels swallow vegetation whole and store it in the first stomach chamber. Here, bacteria attack the food and break it down. Later, when resting, camels cough up a cud of this undigested food and chew it thoroughly by passing it back and forth from one side of the mouth to the other. After being masticated, the cud is reswallowed and passed to the other stomach compartments where gastric juices complete the digestive process and reduce food to a watery pulp.

CAMELS AND WATER

The average person is convinced that camels store water in their humps and stomachs. This is not true. Nevertheless, from ancient times to the present, storytellers have spun yarns detailing how travelers, lost in the desert, were saved from dying of thirst by killing a camel and drinking the water in its stomach.

Not only tellers of tales have kept this myth alive. For nineteen hundred years, zoologists unquestioningly accepted the report of Pliny the Elder, a famous Roman author-naturalist. In his *Historia Naturalis*, Pliny stated that camels have the ability to store water and draw against it when needed.

In the early 1950's zoologists learned that Pliny had erred. At that time, working under the auspices of UNESCO, Doctors Bodil and Knut Schmidt-Nielsen made the first complete study of camel physiology. Not only did this husband-and-wife team employ such simple devices as measuring the water given to their test animals and weighing the beasts before and after watering but also they engaged in complicated analytical studies. By the time the Schmidt-Nielsens had finished their research they had collected more data about the function of the camel's organs "than had been gathered during the nineteen hundred years since Pliny made his error."

Although the Schmidt-Nielsens proved that camels do not

Camels can go for long periods without water.

store water, they confirmed the belief that drinking the contents of a camel's stomach would keep one from dying of thirst. The fluid in the stomach is not water, however, but a combination of digestive juices and liquified, masticated food. While this mixture is vile smelling and most unappetizing, it does contain enough moisture to revitalize a human suffering from dehydration.

Camels may not store water but they do have the ability to go without drinking for long periods. In North Africa, camels turned out to graze during the winter, when rains keep vegetation fresh and green, refrain from drinking for three or four months. However, there are exceptions to the general rule that camels do not require a constant supply of water. Bawatins, a breed of one-humped camels raised in Oman, an independent state in the Arabian peninsula, demand daily waterings. All camels kept in pens and fed dry food must be watered every two weeks.

Other factors besides the moisture content of their food determine whether or not camels need water. These include the season of the year, brightness of the sun, wind velocity, temperature, the weight being carried, the animal's speed, and the number of hours it travels daily.

Unless dehydrated a camel will not drink. When it does drink, it only replaces the liquid lost since its last drink. This can be a tremendous amount. The Schmidt-Neilsens report that a camel they acquired from a caravan was so emaciated that its ribs stuck out and it could hardly stand. But after drinking twenty-seven gallons of water in ten minutes, the animal was completely refreshed, although its body looked bloated. Tests revealed that within two days the water was evenly distributed and had restored blood, bodily fluids, and cells to their normal water balance.

ADAPTIONS TO HEAT AND COLD

Bactrian camels tolerate temperatures that range from –20° F. to over 100° F. Meanwhile, Arabian camels can cope with extremely high temperatures. Their woolly coats protect them from direct sun and the heat reflected from the sand, and also keep out the heat in the air. Then, too, the wool prevents a camel's sweat from evaporating quickly. Thus, although camels perspire very little, the slow evaporation of their sweat helps cool the body. A camel's long legs also aid in keeping it cool because currents of air can pass across the underparts. Moreover, camels expose as little of their bodies as possible to the direct rays of the sun. When resting they kneel lengthwise to the sun's rays and tuck the legs under the body.

Besides withstanding higher temperatures than humans, camels have a greater tolerance to dehydration. Camels, dehydrated when crossing deserts, may lose water equal to 30 percent of their body weight without suffering harm. But a human who loses 12 to 15 percent of his body fluid dies. This is because humans lose most of their water from the blood. As

Camels kneel lengthwise to the sun's rays to keep cool. Some camels enjoy a swim.

a result, the heart becomes overtaxed in its attempt to pump the blood. But a dehydrated camel's blood suffers only a slight water loss, although the animal loses considerable water from its tissue. Since there is no strain on the heart, the camel's body processes are not slowed down.

One of the main reasons camels can tolerate heat is their wide temperature range. In the morning a camel's temperature may be as low as 93° F. but it may rise as high as 104° F. during the heat of the day. This means that camels absorb far less heat from their surroundings than man, whose temperature normally remains at a constant 98.6° F. Meanwhile, as its temperature rises, a camel stores up heat in its body. This heat is slowly released through the skin during the cool of the night.

49

4
A MOST USEFUL BEAST

"But a Camel comes handy
Wherever it's sandy . . ."—Carryl

There is much to be said in favor of the camel. It can carry a heavy load, draw a plow or a wagon, be bartered for goods, serve as part payment for a wife, comprise part of a dowry, and furnish food, clothing, and shelter.

A SOURCE OF FOOD AND CLOTHING

Although butter can be churned from camel's milk, some desert peoples use melted fat from the hump in place of butter. The rich milk, which is so thick that it congeals into lumps when poured into tea or coffee, is made into cheese throughout the Middle East. It is easier to make butter and cheese from the milk of the Bactrian camel, but the Somali of East Africa produce huge amounts of butter and cheese from the Arabian camel's milk. The Somali, who measure an individual's wealth by the number of camels he owns, are dairy farmers who raise camels rather than cattle. Camel's milk is a staple food in their diet.

50

Milking a Mongolian camel. Note the raggedy coat.

This is particularly true when the men live alone in herding camps. The only pack camels these tribesmen possess are a few head used to carry the poles that form the framework of a Somali dwelling.

Middle Eastern tradition demands that the hump of a camel be served to honored guests. But the Roman emperor Elagabalus (A.D. 218–222) preferred camel-foot stew. Some modern camel owners praise his taste. Others do not. Still others find even the thought of eating camel abhorrent. Actually, man's attitude toward eating camel meat varies from one locale to another. The

Tuaregs, outstanding breeders of camels, never eat it. But *bastourma*, sliced grilled camel meat flavored with garlic, has long been considered a delicacy in Armenia.

Camels are an important food source for many desert tribes, which regularly slaughter young animals for their veal-like flesh. Other nomads never kill and eat a camel except on extremely important occasions. Some tribesmen observe the ancient custom of killing the tenth calf to be borne by a female camel and then serving it at a feast which only men attend. Meanwhile, the calf's mother is marked so that she will never be ridden again.

For centuries, the soft wool of the camel—which is gathered from the ground and bushes during the molting season—has been handwoven into cloth and blankets. Because of its length and thickness, the wool of Bactrians is preferred by commercial weavers. But Bedouins have no difficulty weaving clothing and tenting from Arabian camel's wool. Camel's-hair cloth is manufactured in factories, and this cloth is tailored into expensive suits and coats. Moreover, the camel's tough skin furnishes a strong leather from which saddles, sandals, and water bags are fashioned.

Primitive peoples hacked crude utensils out of dried camel bones. Today, skilled craftsmen carve the bones, which resemble ivory, into exquisite jewelry. Visitors to art museums admire pictures painted with camel's hair brushes while Bedouin families, chilled by the cool desert night, huddle around fires made with dried camel dung.

UNPOPULAR AND UNWANTED

Because men use the camel for so many purposes, it seems strange, at first thought, that early, agriculturally based civilizations took so long to adopt it. As indicated, traders had made the animal a familiar sight in the Near and Middle East at a very

Caravans carrying goods to and from the ancient city of Acre rested in this inn (khan) on the shores of the Mediterranean. Today, it is surrounded by homes and shops, some of which date back to the Middle Ages.

early date. So had the warrior kings, whose camelry galloped over many a foot soldier. Yet history reveals that both city merchants and the farmers who practiced irrigation in the river valleys hesitated to adopt the camel.

There was good reason. Not only is the camel bad-tempered but also it is difficult to train, as it does not have much intelligence. Moreover, camels stink. This is why Roman garrisons tethered their camels far from their encampments. Such an arrangement would be impractical in an urban community but few city dwellers could tolerate the stench from camels stabled nearby. In addition, a camel's odor is far more offensive to horses and other domesticated animals than it is to man. Stock not trained to accept the strange scent of the camel becomes uncontrollable. Therefore, in general, it is impossible to quarter camels and farm animals together.

Actually, camels were a bad investment for farmers. Where the climate permitted cattle-raising, the humidity made camels susceptible to a number of diseases. Although camels throve on vegetation other animals could not eat, they had to graze over a wide area to get enough food. This was impossible in ancient times when agriculture was confined to small plots.

Nor was it economical for farmers who had plenty of fodder to pen camels and stall-feed them. There was far more profit in raising animals that could be bred at least once a year. Camels, unlike the majority of domesticated animals, are slow to breed. Female camels are not sexually mature until they are five years old and can only have one calf every two years.

THE DESERT TRADE

Although camels were not stabled inside ancient cities, they were a familiar sight as they plodded through the narrow winding streets, bearing goods to the marketplace. A camel train was always warmly welcomed by local merchants who were eager to see what wares it had brought from a distant point. However, few of the merchants' customers stopped to think that the only reason they could purchase wares from cities on the other side of a mountain range or across a desert was because the camel had been domesticated.

The camel drivers of yesteryear realized that they would work their animals to death if they forced them to carry too much weight. Thus, they usually limited a load to about 500 pounds. Today, a camel's burden ranges from 439 pounds to 1200 pounds. One of the most unusual cargoes ever carried by "ships of the desert" was an extremely heavy load. It consisted of bronze salvaged from the Colossus of Rhodes. Overthrown by an earthquake, this huge statue of the sun god lay untouched for over four hundred years. In A.D. 656, an enterprising mer-

Section of a bas-relief from the royal palace at Nimrud showing an Arab queen surrendering to the Assyrians and leading a train of captured camels.

chant loaded the bronze on nine hundred camels and took it to Syria, where it was made into lamps.

Because it was most profitable to load camels with small items of great value, the articles carried by most caravans were similar to those packed by the camels that accompanied the Queen of Sheba when she visited King Solomon. Her Majesty's animals ". . . bore spices and much gold and precious stones." Camel trains also transported incense, porcelains, silks, rugs, and hand-wrought metal objects.

It is fascinating to conjure up the sights, sounds, and scents of the mysterious East by recalling the days when tiny tinkling bells announced the arrival of a caravan. But the thousands of camels that carried dried dates and such utilitarian articles as pots and pans must not be forgotten. Their loads did not contain treasures but they did help make the "desert trade" economically important.

Although cities along ancient trade routes did not permit caravans to stable their camels inside their walls, they honored the animals that made them rich by placing representations of the camel on coins.

Certain cities on caravan routes became bustling centers of commerce and acquired great wealth. Many of these communities honored the animal that made them rich by placing a camel on their coins even though they continued to ban the stabling of camels inside their walls.

No cities were more prosperous than those along the Persia-to-China trade route. The Bactrian camels that packed goods across deserts, steppes, and towering ranges were hardy creatures. Their ability to endure cold, thirst, and hunger while carrying heavy loads through mountain passes was recognized by the compiler of an early Sanskrit dictionary. He gives a glowing description of the "two humped (camel) capable of crossing difficult passes."

But despite the widespread use of the camel as a pack animal, wheeled vehicles gave it keen competition during the first five hundred years of the Christian era. Most traders carted their goods in wagons drawn by oxen over the well-built roads constructed by rulers of city-states and Roman emperors. Only rarely was the camel employed as a draft animal.

Camel vs Cart

Transporting goods from one city to another by camel train was a risky venture. Caravans not only encountered hardships but also had to defend themselves from robber tribesmen mounted on swifter camels. Eventually, traders learned that the easiest way to stop these raids was to pay tribute to the Arabs who organized them. This arrangement worked quite well until the Arabs decided they could accumulate far more wealth by engaging in the desert trade than by selling "protection." In time they controlled most caravan routes and ruled over many important market cities.

To increase their profits, the Arabs placed a high tax on loads foreign traders transported in wheeled vehicles drawn by oxen. For example, the duty on a wagonload of merchandise brought into the city of Palmyra in Syria was equal to the fee charged for bringing four loaded camels inside the walls. When the Romans invaded Palmyra and captured its ruler Queen Zenobia —who unsuccessfully attempted to flee the city on camelback— they raised the tax on wagons.

It was not only taxes that led to an increased use of the camel as a pack animal. When Rome fell, the network of roads that had connected that city with its colonies fell into disrepair. Within a short time many of them could not be used by wheeled vehicles.

A Chinese camel cart plying between Kalgan and Urga

The old in transportation meets the new.

Thus the demand for pack animals grew. It was met by nomadic tribesmen who had raised camels for years—each tribe confident that the animals it bred were superior to all others.

BREEDING CAMELS

As indicated, male camels are very disagreeable. But their normal conduct is faultless compared to their actions during the mating season. Not only are they dangerous to man at this time but also they kick, bite, and wrestle their rivals for a female's attention. When not fighting they stalk about hoping to attract a potential mate by making a gurgling sound that resembles "water running out of a bath." Courting males also try to impress females by inflating their tongues "until they hang out like pink balloons."

Female camels carry their young for 370 to 440 days. Only a single calf is born, twins being exceptionally rare. Except for its teeth, lack of callosities, and an undeveloped hump, a baby camel is a miniature of its parents. However, a baby camel's thick, woolly fleece is much softer than that of an adult camel.

Born with its eyes open a baby camel can stand almost immediately and is able to run when only a few hours old. If hungry or frightened, it calls its mother with a lamblike *baa*. Because female camels are more tractable than males, camel breeders usually kill all but a few males at birth.

Camels are excellent mothers. Females care for their offspring until they are about four years old. Then, suddenly, a mother will ignore her baby. If the youngster insists upon her attention she drives it away by nipping its flanks. In many cases the young camel responds to the nips with a vicious kick before it leaves.

Selective mating has developed numerous breeds of camels. Perhaps the most graceful and streamlined is the Majari, a camel

This baby Bactrian is wrapped in felt to protect it from the winter's cold.

raised by the Tuaregs, the most advanced of desert peoples. Equally outstanding are the pack and draft camels developed by the Baluchi of western Pakistan who are recognized as the most important camel breeders east of Arabia.

Although the list of camel breeds is a long one, in general most camels raised for market have always been run-of-the-herd stock. Meanwhile, the increased use of trucks designed for desert travel has greatly reduced the demand for camels in recent years. But before the outbreak of World War I, Egypt alone imported approximately 32,000 camels every year from Syria and Arabia.

SADDLE AND HARNESS

Properly handled, camels equal oxen as draft animals. They were used to pull plows throughout the Near East. This practice began with the farmers who lived near Lepcis Magna, the northern terminal of the trans-Sahara trade route on the Mediterranean coast. Although these men knew nothing of the camel gear of the Far East, they devised a camel harness. By making improvements to this tack they were able to harness two camels together or to team a camel and a donkey—a combination still used to till soil in North Africa.

North African farmers were not alone in seeking a suitable

Note the horse collars on this team of camels pictured about fifty years

This unusual stereopticon view shows a camel harnessed to a lawnmower in Central Park in New York City, about 1868.

camel harness. Over the years, drought and soil-eroding farming practices reduced the amount of agricultural land throughout the Near East. As a result, farmers whose fields could no longer support oxen began to use camels. But rigging a harness for the camel was no easy task. Its conformation does not permit using the same gear employed to hitch the donkey, horse, or mule to a wagon. Moreover, it is quite difficult to attach an ox yoke to a camel's elongated neck. In time, various types of harness were developed to meet special needs. One of the most common— used to hitch camels to wheeled vehicles—consisted of straps attached to shafts on either side of the animal's body, the shafts being held in place by other straps fastened across the back.

Like harness makers, saddle designers had to contend with the hump. Experience had taught them that it was almost im-

ago while helping to build a dam to water sheep in New South Wales.

A practical camel saddle—framework forms box around the hump.

possible to secure a heavy load to the hump and, further, the hump became deformed if subjected to excessive weight.

Eventually, three major types of camel saddles (all of which had local variants) evolved. The first type was fastened in front of the hump. This arrangement gave a rider constant control of his mount—it could be guided by the pressure of toes on the neck. Another advantage of this saddle was that, when used to carry a load, the weight was borne by the camel's shoulders. The second type of saddle, which was placed behind the hump, put the weight on the animal's back. Tribesmen who used this type of saddle directed their mounts with sticks.

The most practical saddle originated in northern Arabia. Its framework forms a box around the hump and rests on pads. Riders sit on the top of the frame (which is also padded), their weight evenly distributed to both sides of the camel's rib cage. When a north Arabian saddle is used to pack a load, camel drivers divide the load equally and lash each half to opposite sides of the frame.

Not only did the development of the north Arabian saddle increase the camel's value as a mount and pack animal but also it changed the tactics of camel-riding warriors. The frame gave them the advantage of height and thus enabled them to use spears and long swords when battling an unmounted foe.

5

THE CAMEL IN WAR

". . . And used to war's alarms . . ."—Hood

Sheiks who led camel-riding peoples could make their tribes wealthy in three ways. They could engage in racketeering and offer the caravans that passed through their lands "protection," take an active part in the transdesert trade, or wage war on their farming neighbors. Many tribal leaders chose war. Mounting their followers on speedy dromedaries, they led them far and wide, looting and collecting tribute as they rode.

RAIDERS ON CAMELBACK

Certain peoples became rich by alternating between selling goods and waging war. Among these were the Midianites who were not only involved in the Arabian gold and incense trade but also in the transportation of goods between Syria and Egypt. Skilled in the breeding of camels, the Midianites frequently invaded ancient Israel from the eastern desert. According to the scribe who compiled the Book of Judges in the Old Testament, the Midianites streamed into the Holy Land about 1100 B.C. and

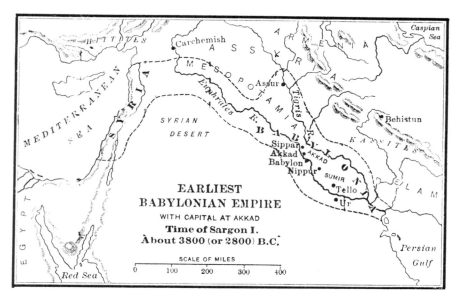

Old map of the earliest Babylonian Empire

". . . their camels were without numbers; and they entered the land to destroy it."

Because of the lack of evidence we can only guess where and when camels were first used in warfare. However, we do know that Sargon I who ruled over Akkad (the northern division of ancient Babylonia) in 2400 B.C. extended his empire by the use of camelry. Historians have also determined that camel-mounted troops were a fixture of Arab armies a thousand years before the birth of Christ. Meanwhile, other people employed camels to carry military supplies. Perhaps the most unusual load packed by any army's camels was the one borne by the animals owned by Sammu-ramat, queen of Assyria. It consisted of disassembled boats which, when put together, enabled Her Majesty's troops to cross rivers far from guarded bridges and fords.

By the ninth century B.C., the Assyrians were constantly battling camel-riding warriors. In every campaign the Assyrians were at a disadvantage. This was because they were convinced that the camel was of no military value except as a pack animal. Thus, when fighting the Arabs who used camels as a platform from which to shoot arrows, the Assyrians rode horses or drove chariots. As a result, even if they won a victory on the battlefield, the Assyrians could not take full advantage of their success. The retreating raiders made for the desert where neither horse nor chariot could overtake their dromedaries.

Nevertheless, the Assyrian assessment of the camel as a mount for soldiers has considerable merit. Camels cannot produce the momentum and impact of galloping war-horses. Therefore a charge made by conventional cavalry has far more power than one made by camelry. This is the reason why tribesmen from the desert borderlands often rode camels to a battlefield, then mounted horses. While the switch increased the fierceness of their attack, it deprived them of the one advantage a camel rider has over a horseman—a higher seat. The development of the north Arabian saddle not only raised camel troops even higher but also, as indicated, paved the way for camelry to attack with spear and long sword.

Assyrian chariot from a bas-relief. The height of a camel gave the camelry an advantage in battle.

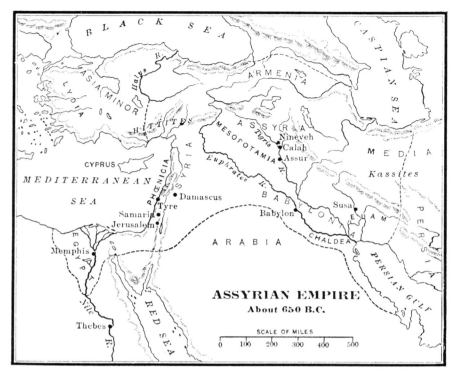

Assyrian Empire about 650 B.C.

Eventually, the great Assyrian king Assurbanipal established a camel corps which soundly defeated the Arabs in a series of battles. The victorious Assyrians brought a tremendous amount of loot back to Nineveh, including hundreds of dromedaries and pack camels. As a result, a camel could be bought for a few cents in most Assyrian marketplaces. This was not solely due to the great number of camels offered for sale. The average Assyrian had little use for a camel.

EARLY CAMEL CORPS

Most monarchs in the East had camel-riding troops. But none could boast of as large a force as the Great Mogul Akbar who commanded twelve thousand warriors fighting on camels. Akbar never compiled a battle plan without considering how his camelry could be used most effectively. On the other hand, Cyrus the Great, supreme ruler of the Medes and Persians, never employed camels on the battlefield until his army clashed with the host led by Croesus, king of Lydia, at the Battle of Sardis in 564 B.C. Herodotus explains why Cyrus decided to use camels:

> When Cyrus beheld the Lydians arranging themselves in order of battle . . . fearful of the strength of their cavalry, he adopted a device. . . . He collected together all the camels which had come in the train of his army to carry the provisions and the baggage, and taking off their loads he mounted riders upon them accoutred as horsemen. These he commanded to advance in front of his other troops against the Lydian horse. . . . The reason why Cyrus opposed his camels to the enemy's horse was because the horse has a natural dread of the camel, and cannot abide either the sight or smell of that animal. . . . The two

LEFT: *Bas-relief of Cyrus the Great.*
BELOW: *Persian foot soldiers.*

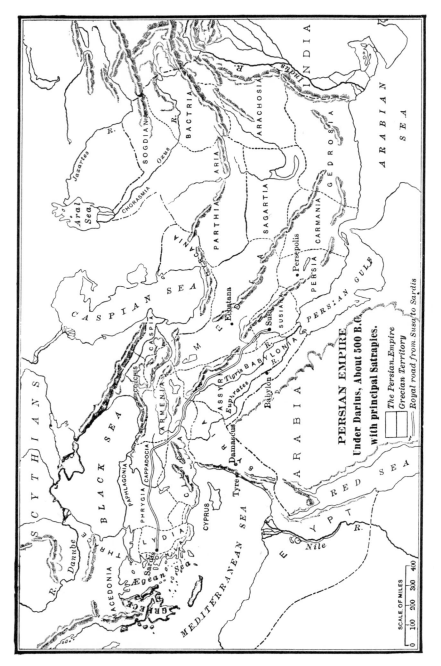

The Persian Empire under Darius, about 500 B.C.

armies then joined battle and immediately the Lydian war-horses, seeing and smelling the camels, turned around and galloped off; and so it came to pass that all Croesus' hopes withered away.

Following the victory at Sardis, Cyrus established a camel corps in the Persian army. Originally, its ranks were filled by recruits from conquered lands but eventually it was composed of Arab mercenaries. After the death of Alexander the Great, the Greeks also hired Arab camelry armed with swords six feet long. However, the Roman emperors Hadrian and Trajan employed the practice of enlisting conquered peoples in the camel corps they organized in Egypt and Syria.

At first, Roman camelry engaged in such simple duties as patrolling borders and protecting caravans but soon became an important part of the imperial army. In order to insure an ample supply of mounts and pack animals, Roman officials demanded camels as tribute from captured towns. Thus, in A.D. 363, four thousand camels were requisitioned from the town of Lepcis Magna. But their delivery did not cause as much excitement as had the arrival in Rome of the twenty-six dromedaries Julius Caesar had taken from the Numidians in 46 B.C.

MODERN CAMEL CORPS

Theoretically, development of the cannon should have driven camels from the battlefield. However, camels continued to carry soldiers and to transport artillery. The seventeenth-century Turks were probably the first to mount cannon on camels. By the late eighteenth century it was a common practice. Among the unusual field pieces loaded on camels and fired from their backs were "falconets"—small cannons used by the Afghans in their war against the Persians in 1772. Falconets were not only

Lawrence of Arabia, who led the desert tribes against the Turks in World War I. Few modern military heroes had such a colorful and romantic career as Colonel Thomas E. Lawrence of the British Army.

light in weight but also were fastened to a pivot which permitted aiming them in any direction.

Napoleon organized a camel corps and used it for reconnaissance during his Egyptian campaign. Interestingly enough, camels contributed to Napoleon's downfall—the Russian troops who marched on Paris in 1814 used camels to pack baggage. But these were not the first camels to accompany an army in Europe. The Goths who conquered the Danube Basin not only rode horses but also camels they had captured in Mongolia.

In 1844, a high-ranking French officer suggested that a camel corps be created in Algeria (then a French colony). However, it was not until 1895 that French troops were mounted on camels and assigned to patrol the desert. That same year a British camel corps distinguished itself during the War of the Sudan.

Because the camel has great strength and the ability to go without food and water for long periods, modern military men prefer it to all other beasts of burden with the possible exception of the mule. But they have not always been successful in their attempts to convince their governments to employ camels as pack animals. Even the British army which used camels in Africa and India could not be persuaded to adopt them in other areas.

Meanwhile, as early as 1837, American Army officers were advocating using camels as transport. But it was not until 1855 that the Congress, prodded by Secretary of War Jefferson Davis (later president of the Confederacy) approved the importation of camels. The animals were used by units surveying possible

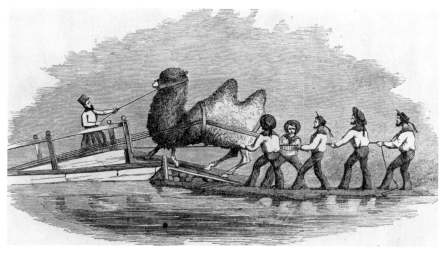

Although the Congress approved the importation of camels for use by Army units just before the War Between the States, the task of loading the animals aboard ship and transporting them to the United States was assigned to the Navy.

wagon routes from the Southwest and Nevada to California. They were also given the task of carrying supplies to the army posts that protected travelers and settlers from the Indians.

The camel experiment was very successful. Nevertheless, the army's use of camels came to an end because of the outbreak of the War Between the States. After the war ended, Americans turned to railroads rather than camels to open up the West. The government sold its camels to owners of circuses or to individuals who used the animals to carry ore and to haul freight. Most of these enterprises failed and the camels were turned loose. As a result, accounts of a camel being sighted in Arizona or New Mexico frequently appeared in newspapers until the 1920's. But for every camel actually seen, a dozen tall tales were told about a huge camel that galloped across the Great

Old print of a camel train in Nevada

Fantasma Colorado as pictured by Ted Lewin, from the book Ghostly Animals of America *by Patricia Edwards Clyne*

American Desert with a man's skeleton on its back.

Although the camel was rejected by the United States Army over a century ago, many Americans who served in the armed forces during World War II can recall the camels that carried supplies to remote outposts in the wilds of Burma and India. However, the number of camels used for military purposes during World War II was very small compared to the number employed during World War I. Approximately three million camels served in World War I while only some fifty thousand were enlisted in World War II.

6
THE CAMEL'S FUTURE

"... meat for the hungry ..."—Cervantes

Over the centuries man has attempted to introduce the camel into many countries. In most instances he has failed. However there have been some notable successes. Perhaps the greatest was in Australia.

Camels were first imported by Australians in the mid-nineteenth century. Originally, they were used to carry supplies for the expeditions that explored the "outback"—the rugged interior of the island continent—but eventually they were employed to transport goods and to pull farm equipment. By 1925, thousands of camels were serving Australian masters. Today, because of the development of the truck and mechanized farm machinery, camels are of little use to Australians. In fact, the estimated twenty thousand feral camels—descendants of the animals imported from India—that roam the outback are considered "vermin." This is because they knock down fences and compete with livestock for food and water.

However, the Northern Territorial Police Force uses camels for patrols in the trackless country of the hinterland. Camel rid-

An Australian traffic hazard. This young feral camel from the Outback likes to walk down the white line that divides a major highway.

ing is also a highly popular tourist attraction in central Australia where camels are being bred from descendants of the stock that was allowed to run wild after the introduction of railroads and automobiles "down under."

Recently Robyn Davison, a young Australian, retraced the route of early camel-riding explorers and crossed Australia's arid western region with four camels. Although Miss Davison's caravan (and the feral camels she encountered) caused her considerable trouble during her 1700-mile trek, she maintains that despite its evil reputation the camel is "most loveable."

It is not only in Australia that machinery has replaced the camel. Even in the Near and Middle East—long the centers of

75

A jaunt on camelback across the Australian Outback

camel breeding—the roar of trucks and the whine of tractors can be heard. Nevertheless, in some areas the camel is still indispensable. Therefore the State of Rajasthan in India is developing a strain of camels capable of hauling exceptionally heavy loads across the Great Indian Desert.

Generally speaking, despite the Rajasthan project and similiar programs, the camel's value as a beast of burden has declined. But a number of scientists are convinced that the camel will continue to serve man in the future. These individuals claim that camel raising is an "obvious solution to the need of increased meat production" in a world whose ever increasing population demands more food yearly.

The idea of raising large numbers of camels for meat has considerable merit. As indicated, because camels eat vegetation unpalatable to other domesticated animals, camel ranching would make desert land now unfit for agriculture productive. Moreover, the camel's ability to go without water enables it to range far greater distances in search of food than sheep or cattle. As a result, camels are ideal "livestock" in areas that have been overgrazed. Thus there is little doubt that eventually an international commission will devise techniques for raising, butchering, and shipping camel meat in order to help feed the world's hungry peoples.

INDEX

SIGMUND A. LAVINE was highly active while in college; he wrote features for the *Boston Sunday Post* and covered Boston University sports for two wire services. After receiving his M.A., he taught in a United States Government Indian School at Belcourt, North Dakota, for two years, learning to speak both the Sioux and Cree languages and talk in sign language. He was invited to tribal dances, ceremonies, and Indian Court in reservations throughout Canada and the Northwest.

Sigmund Lavine has taught in the Boston schools for over thirty years and is now an assistant principal. He also lectures and writes literary criticism.

He lives with his wife in a house filled with books, fish tanks, historical china, art glass, and the largest privately owned collection of Gilbert and Sullivan material in America. For relaxation the Lavines attend country auctions, go "antiquing," or browse in bookstores, but their greatest pleasure is truck gardening on a piece of rocky New Hampshire land.